Original title:

Palm Tree Dreams

Copyright © 2025 Creative Arts Management OÜ
All rights reserved.

Author: Dexter Sullivan
ISBN HARDBACK: 978-1-80581-691-1
ISBN PAPERBACK: 978-1-80581-218-0
ISBN EBOOK: 978-1-80581-691-1

Paradise Found

In a land where coconuts roll,
And seagulls play a silly stroll,
I found a hat stuck on a dog,
As I danced with a wobbly frog.

Beneath a sky of cotton candy,
I discovered the sun was quite dandy,
With flip-flops singing on my feet,
And a crab trying to dance to the beat.

Voyage of Warm Winds

I sailed on a breeze called Giggle Gale,
With a ship made of ice cream and a jelly whale,
All the birds wore shades and did a shimmy,
As the waves played jokes; oh, how they made me zippy.

The clouds were marshmallows, fluffy and grand,
While I swam with fish that spoke in rhyme and planned,
To tickle the sun with a feather on a kite,
And toast to the fun that lasted all night.

The Call of the Sun-Drenched Isles

The islands called with a goofy song,
With pineapples dancing, how could I go wrong?
The monkeys were trading their jokes for bananas,
While the beaches performed in their colorful planners.

A crab in a tuxedo led a parade,
Waving at tourists, unafraid,
While the sun tickled the horizon wide,
And the tides couldn't stop their giggling ride.

Stories in the Sand

On grains of gold, tales twist and twirl,
As sea turtles breakdance—what a whirl!
The shells whispered secrets from a comical past,
While sea stars plotted their next funny cast.

With every wave, laughter flies high,
As fish wear hats and wave goodbye,
The sandcastle kings throw a wild bash,
In a world where giggles and dreams splash.

Underneath Tropical Skies

Beneath bright clouds, a party's near,
Sipping coconut water, loud and clear.
The sun a clown in a golden suit,
While seagulls dance, in their wacky route.

Cocktails in hand, we jig and jive,
A conga line, that's oh so alive!
With sticky feet in the sand we sway,
Blame it on the heat, hey, what can I say?

Echoing Laughter on the Breeze

Tickling winds whisper jokes to the palm,
A coconut falls, when it's too calm.
A parrot squawks, it joins our cheer,
"Is it happy hour? I'm ready, my dear!"

The crabs do a dance, so absurdly grand,
While we cheer them on, maracas in hand.
The sun takes a break, starts to waddle,
As we burst forth laughing, it struts like a model.

Cascades of Green

Leaves cascading, what a sight to behold,
A toucan's fashion, bright and bold.
We mimic its calls, in silly tones,
Echoes of laughter rise, like playful drones.

Goofy sunburns form patterns we wear,
Our ice cream melts, no worries, no care.
Rolling in sunbeams, with no hint of strife,
Each giggle a splash of our vivid life.

Tides of Tranquility

Waves roll in with a tickle and tease,
Shells laugh at strangers, with giggling ease.
We float on our backs, hats drifting away,
A friendly crab joins, claims he's here to stay.

Every splash a chorus, the sea sings too,
Mixing salt and absurdity in the blue.
While all our worries catch waves on the shore,
We dance 'til the sunset, forever, encore!

Whispers of the Tropical Sky

A monkey in a hat does sway,
He thinks he's hip, at least today.
With coconuts, he starts to dance,
While all the cows just stare in trance.

The parrots squawk, it's quite a show,
Sipping fruit juice, on the go.
The breeze carries laughter all around,
As flip-flops splash on sandy ground.

Shadows Beneath the Sun

Sun hats wobble, heads do bob,
While hands get stuck in mango glob.
The shadows tease and play all day,
As flip-flops vanish in the fray.

A crab in shades struts with great flair,
While sunburned tourists catch some air.
With ice cream cones that melt and drip,
They giggle loud and take a trip.

Breeze-Kissed Reveries

A seagull snatches chips with glee,
While penguins waddle down the spree.
The surfboard's lost to a big wave,
And all the kids just laugh and rave.

With swimming rings and silly games,
The fun is driven by wild flames.
Bright umbrellas twirl and fly,
As giggles reach the passing sky.

Sunlit Avenues of Thought

With thoughts adrift in coconut cream,
And ice cream trucks that moo and beam.
The sun can be a sneaky chap,
As shade brings forth a funny clap.

While tourists chase a wayward hat,
A dolphin laughs, and that is that.
A serenade, a breezy tune,
As bright as candy, light as a balloon.

Garden of Forgotten Whispers

In a garden where socks might roam,
Lost to the wild, they're far from home.
Comets in slippers, a sight to behold,
Chasing the shadows, just a bit bold.

A carrot debates with a cheeky bean,
Hilarious chats, where's the routine?
They giggle and wiggle under the sun,
As ladybugs dance, having too much fun.

A frog in a hat sings a silly song,
It croaks about right, but it's always wrong.
The daisies are laughing, can't hold their glee,
At pitches so high, only birds can see.

So if you find laughter in your backyard,
Join in the folly, it's never too hard.
Whispers of giggles in leaves all around,
In this whimsical space, joy is found.

Hushed Murmurs of the Sands

A grain of sand wears a tiny crown,
It quips and jokes as it rolls around.
The waves applaud with a thunderous cheer,
As crabs tell tales that we can't quite hear.

Turtles that surf on the crest of a wave,
Making a splash, they're so very brave.
Seagulls exchange their best gossiping tips,
As hidden beach parties give scandalous flips.

Starfish in shades, lounging on the shore,
They gossip about the ocean's great lore.
With jokes that are deep, they're creatures of wit,
As the tide's tickled, it can't help but split.

So when you wander where laughter is loud,
Join in the fun, be goofy and proud.
Among the soft whispers of waves in the night,
Find joy in the sand, let your heart take flight.

The Nature of Serenity

A cactus once dreamed of dancing with stars,
It shook all its needles, and watched from afar.
With a sway and a twist, it gave quite a show,
While the tumbleweeds giggled, 'Look at it go!'

The clouds all chuckled, sharing a grin,
At the sight of the cactus trying to spin.
Winds wrapped around like a friend's warm embrace,
As nature applauded this whimsical place.

Trees had a party, with raucous delight,
Their branches were swaying with all of their might.
Squirrels in tuxedos served acorns like wine,
While barking dogs barked, "This humor's divine!"

And if you can hear that soft rustling song,
Join in the laughter; it won't steer you wrong.
In the nature surrounding, you'll find your own glee,
A harmony woven in life's comedy.

Visions of Coastal Calm

A fish in a bowler sits sipping some tea,
Says, "Ever tried swimming while sipping with me?"
With bubbles and giggles, it tells quite a tale,
Of seahorses dancing in a shimmering veil.

A clam jokes with shells about current events,
They chuckle at crabs, so very intense.
The dolphins are all on a splashing spree,
Gossiping merrily under the sea.

Breezes are nudging the gulls into flight,
As owls bring their wisdom for a laugh at night.
Jellyfish jiggle, with beams of delight,
In this tranquil place, everything feels right.

So come along to this coastal delight,
Where laughter and fun wrap around you tight.
Amidst all the waves and the laughter-filled balm,
Life dances along in a rhythm so calm.

Dreaming Under Tropical Palms

Beneath the sun, I lay so still,
A sandwich falls, it's quite a thrill.
The seagulls laugh, they steal my fries,
While I just dream of ocean skies.

A crab in shades, he winks at me,
He's got the moves, oh, can't you see?
We dance together on the sand,
I lead the way, it's really grand.

The beach ball bounces, oh so high,
My dog jumps up with a goofy cry.
He steals my hat, he runs with glee,
Life's a party, just him and me.

As sunset colors paint the night,
I chase fireflies, what a delight!
A coconut falls, I duck and weave,
In this sweet dream, I won't believe!

Lifetimes in the Shade

Sipping drinks adorned with fruit,
The lazy cat digs in the loot.
She dreams of fish, she purrs and sprawls,
While I just chuckle at her brawls.

The hammock sways, I rock about,
I stretch a limb and hear a shout.
A parrot squawks, he gets a snack,
A lifetime spent, no need to pack.

A lizard poses on a chair,
He steals the show with his green flair.
He flicks his tongue, he looks so sly,
While I just plan my next lie by.

Beneath the leafy, swaying boughs,
I make my peace with silly vows.
To laugh forever in the shade,
Where even worries start to fade.

Mirage of Coastal Visions

The waves go crashing, fish parade,
I wear my fins, I'm a mermaid.
With goofy grace, I splash about,
A dolphin laughs, I hear him shout.

When jellybeans fall from the sky,
I grab my net—oh me, oh my!
The tide pulls back, it's quite a scene,
With every giggle, things get mean.

The sandcastles rise, they slump and drop,
With seashells gathered, never stop.
A pail in hand, I'm quite the pro,
But my royal tower just said, "No!"

As seagulls squabble for my fries,
They've formed a team—quite the surprise.
I hold my ground; I shall not yield,
In this mirage, my joy is sealed!

Coconut Wishes in the Breeze

A coconut falls, I duck and dive,
It bounces round, it's quite alive.
I laugh and spin, what a wild show,
With palm fronds swaying to and fro.

The tides bring in a playful tide,
I build a boat, my trusty bride.
Made of driftwood, it looks so neat,
But it's just a raft for my pet's feet.

The sun sets low, the night's a laugh,
I roast some marshmallows, that's my craft.
A raccoon joins, he steals the s'mores,
He's got the moves; I can't ignore.

With wishes blown into the air,
I dream of fun without a care.
In this light-hearted island spree,
The breeze carries our giggles, free!

The Ascent of Tender Green

In the sun, they stretch and sway,
No need for haircuts, come what may!
Leaves high-five the fluffy clouds,
Whispers hang, and laughter shrouds.

Squirrels dance like they own the place,
Strutting about with dubious grace.
A breeze nudges, they tilt and lean,
What a sight, a quirky scene!

With coconuts, their fortunes grow,
Shaking them for a cool show.
A thump, a bump – they drop with flair,
Rolling 'round like they just don't care!

So here's to greens that shimmy high,
Underneath the endless sky.
In their shade, the giggles beam,
Life's a joke, or so it seems!

Fiesta of Light and Shadow

Underneath bright beams of sun,
Laughter dances, oh what fun!
Shadows flicker, a game of peek,
Nature's whimsy can't be bleak.

Birds in hats, they strut with pride,
Swinging high with joy, they glide.
Cocktails made of nectar sweet,
Who knew shade could be this neat?

A playful breeze tugs at their feet,
Bringing giggles, oh so sweet.
Mischievous leaves drift down with flair,
Doing the twist without a care!

All around, a festive air,
Nature's party, dress to dare.
Join the fun, lend your cheer,
In this chaos, joy draws near!

Tidal Echoes of Reverie

Waves crash in a rhythm wild,
While seagulls dance, the ocean's child.
Underneath the sun's bright glow,
Sandy feet join in the show.

A splash, a gulp, a funny face,
Tides bring in a dizzying race.
Shells giggle as they tumble down,
As currents swirl, the laughs abound!

Wobbly crabs in their tiny prance,
Join in the merry, beachy dance.
They sidestep waves with silly grace,
Claiming each splash as their new space!

So let the ocean call your name,
In the waves, embrace the game.
Echoes swirl in a playful spree,
As tides whisper joys, wild and free!

Oasis of Forgotten Dreams

In a land where the sun never quits,
Coconuts gossip and share their bits.
Lizards in sunglasses strut their stuff,
While the crabs argue who's tough enough.

Under the shade, where shadows play,
They throw wild parties, come join the fray!
With ocean breeze and a drink in hand,
Life's a cartoon in this goofy land.

Beneath the Lush Canopy

Wobbly monkeys swing from above,
Throwing bananas, it's a labor of love.
Toucan jokes that fly through the air,
While sloths take bets on who really cares.

The parrot squawks a riddle with glee,
But the answer is lost on the tired bee.
They laugh at the clouds, as they float on by,
In the lush canopy, under the bright sky.

Serene Silhouettes Against Dusk

As the sun dips low, shadows dance and sway,
A giraffe in a tux suggests a game of croquet.
Crickets chirp out their evening songs,
While a raccoon claims he knows the throngs.

Fireflies join in, twinkling with flair,
Inviting the grumpy old turtle to share.
But he snores loudly, dreaming of food,
While the rest play on, in a lighthearted mood.

Echoes of Paradise

In the echoing waves, a fish sings a tune,
Of lost sea treasures and a very big moon.
A clam lends an ear, says, "Try a new note!"
While the octopus plays an imaginary boat.

Seagulls join in with their cackling flight,
Making a symphony that feels just right.
And as the sun sets, they frolic with glee,
In a world of dreams, so silly and free.

Twilight Among the Fronds

Underneath the wavy fronds,
Lizards dance in silly ponds.
The sunset blushes, oh so bright,
As squirrels mock the fading light.

Cockatoos with feathers bold,
Tell secrets only they behold.
While crabs in suits swing to and fro,
Claiming the beach as their napping zone.

A parrot juggles all her seeds,
Telling tales filled with silly deeds.
The breeze laughs through the twisted vines,
In twilight where the rum punch shines.

Reflection in the Ocean's Embrace

Reflections shimmer, fish go 'Wow!'
The ocean waves don't know just how.
They crash and giggle on the shore,
Inviting beach balls to explore.

A seagull dives like he's in flight,
Wearing sunglasses, oh what a sight!
He steals my chips, I chase in vain,
While toddlers build their castles, plain.

Sandcastles topple, kids rejoice,
The ocean's bubbles make a noise.
With laughter rippling through the air,
Who knew the tide could be so rare?

Dreamscapes of Sunny Shores

In dreamscapes where the sun is high,
The clouds wear hats, they float on by.
Crabs play poker with the sand,
As kittens lounge, relaxed and grand.

A beach ball hops, it starts to dance,
While flip-flops join in on the chance.
The sand makes jokes, so coarse yet bright,
Under the stars that giggle at night.

So come and join this sunny spree,
Where laughter floats like salt on sea.
In dreams where every wave's a jest,
We'll find the tides that know us best.

Basked in Golden Light

Basked in colors, gold and red,
Beach towels spread like beds instead.
As marshmallows toast upon the sand,
BBQ sauces take a stand!

Seagulls argue over fries,
While sunflowers wear goofy ties.
The sun dips low and starts to sway,
With giggles echoing the day.

A turtle wears a party hat,
Inviting all the critters—chat!
In golden light, we laugh and cheer,
For beach days are the best, my dear!

Tranquil Hues of Dusk

Sunset paints the sky in pink,
Monkeys dance, they nod and wink.
A coconut drops, oh what a sight,
As birds critique in their flight.

Chasing shadows, laughs surround,
Two cats argue on the ground.
Without a care, they flip and roll,
Like beach balls tossed, they've lost control.

Even the fish start to conspire,
With bubbles popping, they're a choir.
Fishes flapping in jubilee,
Who knew the sea could be so free?

Mischief mingles with warm breeze,
Time drips slow, as chill we seize.
In hues of dusk, joy takes the lead,
What a place to let heart's laugh feed.

The Language of Swaying Leaves

The leaves are chatting, what a scene,
With jokes and giggles, oh so keen.
One tipsy branch shakes in a twirl,
Sending a breeze, oh what a whirl!

Squirrels gossip with nuts in hand,
Whirling round to beat the band.
"Hey, did you hear the news today?"
"Only that the sun loves to play!"

A squirrel slips, it's quite the fall,
Bouncing back, it takes a call.
Leaves shiver, flutter, looking grand,
They're all in on this playful band.

Every rustle, a laugh and tease,
This leafy tongue knows how to please.
In the dance of greens, life swings wide,
The humor's bright, there's no need to hide.

Secrets Cradled by the Wind

Whispers travel through the air,
Secrets finding if you're aware.
A gentle breeze, what does it bear?
Oh, tales that tickle without a care.

Bushes chuckle, gossip flows,
Has the wind taken off its clothes?
"Why so bold?" the branches sigh,
As clouds swirl, oh my, oh my!

A raccoon nods, "Let's play charades!"
While grasshopper jumps, clever parades.
Midnight twinkles in a jest,
Charging dreams, this place is blessed.

Secrets fly on this lively ride,
With laughter echoing far and wide.
Nature's giggles, a joyful show,
Where the wind's tune makes spirits glow.

Luminescence of a Starry Night

Stars are winking, it's quite the chat,
A rabbit hops, wearing a hat.
Moon giggles, lighting the way,
Inviting all for a dance and sway.

Fireflies blink, they're off in a chase,
Glowing softly, lights all over the place.
An owl hoots, "Bring on the fun!"
Nighttime shenanigans have just begun.

Crickets chirp, what a loud band,
They're tuning up for the moonlit stand.
With each note, the night takes flight,
Singing silly tunes till morning light.

Under the stars, hilarity reigns,
With laughter spilling through joy's veins.
This dazzling glow, forever delight,
In the magic of the starry night.

Dance of the Island Spirits

In a place where coconuts sway,
The locals laugh through the day.
A dance with a twist and a shout,
You'll find joy in every route.

Crabs wear shades, strut down the sand,
While turtles groove, oh isn't it grand?
Even the fish toss their fins,
For a moment, no one loses or wins.

A parrot chirps, 'More rum!' with a grin,
While conch shells spin like a whirling pin.
The sun sets down with a slip and slide,
As we boogie all night, what a wild ride!

Laughter echoes through the night air,
Under stars with a cheeky flare.
In this realm, all worries cease,
Here's to fun and never a crease.

Enchanted Oasis

In a land where pineapple hats reign,
A sloth sips juice, no hint of pain.
Hammocks swing, as breezes play,
Come join the party, let's sway away!

Lizards skate on slick little stones,
While monkeys throw shade with their phones.
Giggling goats dressed up in styles,
Serve cocktails while balancing smiles.

The flamingos dance with such flair,
Spinning 'round without a care.
A coconut falls, it's a fruity bomb,
But it's all in good fun, call it a charm!

In this place, joy's wild and free,
Every corner begs, "Come dance with me!"
So raise your glass, let's toast to the night,
With laughter and fun, everything's right!

Whispering Winds of Escape

The breeze chuckles through tall green grass,
As iguanas lounge, letting time pass.
With flip-flops flapping, we dash along,
Singing sweet tunes where we all belong.

Seagulls gossip, calling from above,
While crabs bicker, finding their love.
A beach ball bounces, smacking a palm,
It lands on a turtle, who quips, "How calm!"

The sun dips low, skies painted with gold,
As we surf the waves with stories untold.
Fruits and laughter make up our feast,
In this haven, the fun will never cease!

So gather your pals, let's lose all dread,
We'll sip from coconuts, sleep in our bed.
With every soft whisper of wind that we chase,
We'll laugh till dawn, in this magical place!

Beneath the Fronded Halo

Beneath the fronds, where shade is thick,
A crab in a tux performs his trick.
He balances drinks on his tiny claws,
With applause from the crowd, he takes a pause.

The sunbeams tickle our silly toes,
As goats on surfboards strike funny poses.
A turtle rolls in with shades and a grin,
Saying, "The fun's just about to begin!"

With shells as hats, we prance like stars,
While sandcastles rise like tiny bars.
Seashells whisper secrets of cheer,
Promises of laughter, and good times near.

So here's to the quirks of our tropical scene,
With giggles and dreams unclaimed, yet serene.
Let's bask in the joy, and never feel low,
For life's a wild ride, just twist and go!

Fragrant Journeys

On a beach where coconuts fall,
I tried to dance, but took a spill.
The sand it sticks, my toes appall,
I think my grace is gone for good still.

With a breeze that smells of spice,
I tripped and landed on a clam.
It's nice to laugh, but not so nice,
When the ocean waves go 'SPLAM!'

The seagulls mock with their loud cries,
I wave my arms; they think it's neat.
I serenade them, oh-so-wise,
In flip-flops that are far from fleet.

To sail, I planned, with flair so grand,
But forgot the map; I'm lost at sea.
A rubber duck in command,
The captain laughs; he's lost with me.

Revelations Under the Stars

Beneath the moon, I sip my drink,
A straw hat floats right by my head.
I ponder life, then start to think,
Is that my snack, or a fish instead?

A hammock swings, a thrilling ride,
I thought I'd nap, but here I sway.
I wake up grinning, almost fried,
The sun's just laughing at my play.

The fireflies dance; they know I'm here,
I swear they're making jokes at night.
They twinkle in, then disappear,
Is this their way of saying, "Why fight?"

The falling stars, they wink so bright,
With every wish, a giggle splices.
I wish for food at midnight's bite,
And end up treated with more spices!

The Art of Island Living

I threw my line to catch a fish,
Instead, a seaweed wig came back.
I quit that dream, but oh, how I wish,
To dance with dolphins on the track!

A parrot's gossip fills the air,
He tells tall tales of my bad moves.
I bribe him with my easy flair,
And trade for lessons, oh—what grooves!

Each sunset brings a silly show,
The crabs do moonwalks on the sand.
I join the fun, my feet a-blow,
And trip again, oh, isn't it grand?

My island style is full of flair,
With flip-flops, wigs, and shirts too bright.
I wave my arms like I don't care,
While tumbling into a seashell fight!

Ethereal Breezes

In the breeze, I float like air,
A sunscreen spill? It's everywhere!
I try to wave away my hair,
But end up stuck in a sticky pair.

The coconut drinks come with a punch,
I thought I'd sip, but lost my grip.
Now I'm the fruit salad at lunch,
A sunny bowl in a funny trip!

A boat passes, has I spy a cap?
Which lil' kid scoffed at my snooze?
They laugh so hard they make a clap,
While I just float in my lost snooze.

To float or swim, that is my task,
But off I go, no time to ask!
In waves of joy, I wear a mask,
One day, I'll learn it's not a flask!

Dreams of the Distant Shore

In a hammock, I sway with delight,
Imagining coconuts taking flight.
A seagull with glasses, oh what a sight,
Pondering life's questions deep into the night.

Sand castles with moats, ruled by a crab,
He's the king, and I'm just a fab!
Mermaids diving for my missing tab,
While dolphins connect like a social fab!

The waves spill secrets, but only to me,
They chuckle and dance like they're wild and free.
With sunburned cheeks and a bowl of brie,
I toast to the sun, my futuristic glee.

So here's to the shore, with all its charm,
Where laughs are loud and nothing's a harm.
Under the sun, I find my warm,
Dreaming of fish wearing glittering arm!

Invocations of the Tropics

A piña colada, the blender's roar,
Dancing in flip-flops on the grocery floor.
Hula skirts twirl, a quick encore,
As I greet the parrots that my heart adore.

Crabs in sunglasses, strutting by,
They wink at my dance, it's quite the high.
I twirl and giggle, I can't deny,
The sun's my fan, oh me, oh my!

A llama in shorts, prancing so proud,
He joins my conga, draws a little crowd.
Together we laugh; laughter's loud,
In this tropical rain, we're blissfully cowed.

So let the coconuts fall with a splat,
Each hit's a reminder of this goofy chat.
With each sunny day, there's a pitter-pat,
Of laughter and joy—now tell me, how's that?

Lush Divergence

Beneath the sun, I try to dive,
But belly flops make me feel alive!
Fish giggle and ask, 'Can you survive?'
I wave with my snack, hoping they'll thrive.

Laying on grass, I dream of lemonade,
While squirrels debate if they'll invade.
With tiny jester hats, my plans they've laid,
Their antics, like mine, make mammal grade.

Sandy toes poking at seaweed's strand,
As crabs play a game, a bustling band.
Joining their fun, oh isn't it grand?
A party at dusk—it's perfectly planned!

So here in this place, where laughter is spry,
I'll soar with the gulls and dance in the shy.
With dreams made of bubbles that float to the sky,
In hilarity's arms, forever I'll lie!

Memories of a Coastal Haven

A bucket of clams, my treasure's delight,
But they mutter and wiggle—oh, what a fright!
I dance with seaweed, it blooms in the night,
While crabs hold a council, their secret rite.

A tortoise in shades, the coolest I swear,
As he chills by the surf, without a care.
With sunblock in paws, oh the life to compare,
We chat about wanderlust, feelings laid bare.

Waves crash on rocks, like jokes from afar,
Water's punchline makes me a star!
Belly laughs echo, oh my, bizarre,
As I relish the rhythm, my laugh's not ajar.

With sunsets ablaze and laughter in tow,
In this haven of joy, I take it slow.
Let the hype of the world take a little blow,
Here in my heart, the fun will still grow!

Secrets in the Breeze

Whispers dance on sandy shores,
Where birds play tag, and laughter soars.
A coconut drops, the locals shout,
"Watch out below!" They twist and pout.

Flip-flops flop in twilight's glow,
Sipping drinks with lime, oh so slow.
Mischief hides in every breeze,
As gulls steal fries with expert ease.

Sunburned toes wiggle with glee,
While crabs plot schemes that we can't see.
A game of catch, we toss a shoe,
The chase gets fierce, it's quite the view.

And when the night begins to creep,
Seashell secrets start to leap.
Under stars, we laugh and squeal,
For silly moments are the real deal.

Sunlit Blessings

Golden rays and gentle churn,
A beach ball flies, oh how we yearn!
Sandy sandwiches, where's the jam?
Laughter echoes—"That's just a scam!"

In the shade, the ants parade,
While sunburned folks concoct a trade.
"You give me shade, I'll lend you cheer,
But please, no talk of work, my dear."

A seagull swoops to snatch a snack,
We giggle as it turns back,
Uninvited guest, our hands in air,
Funny how it finds us unaware.

With every wave that crashes high,
We dream of flights and coconut pie.
A sunlit afternoon we roam,
In this blissful place we call home.

Elysium Beneath the Palms

Beneath the fronds, a cool retreat,
Where giggles bounce and friends all meet.
A cat naps near, a lazy king,
As we attempt the hula swing.

Bawanana! The smoothie spills,
We dance around, let out our thrills.
A prankster crab steals someone's drink,
We watch and laugh, it makes us wink.

The sun dips low, a fiery hue,
With laughter loud, and gossip too.
A beach bonfire, marshmallow roast,
We toast to life and share a boast.

As shadows grow, our tales do swell,
With every sip, we cast our spell.
Life's untamed joy beneath the shade,
In this paradise, memories are made.

A Symphony of Leaves

Rustling leaves play music sweet,
As breezes swirl, our laughter's fleet.
A squirrel drops acorns down the lane,
We gasp and giggle, 'What a pane!'

Sunlight dances on our skin,
Like nature's wink or playful grin.
A frisbee flies, with silly twirls,
We chase it down, oh how it whirls!

The shade a refuge, stories old,
Of goofy pranks and laughter bold.
Under the shade, we plot and scheme,
In the wild, we chase our dream.

With each new dawn, we start anew,
Adventures waiting just for you.
A symphony of laughter thrives,
In every heart, the joy survives.

Lanterns of the Sunset

Under bright skies, they sway and prance,
A shady dance, a leafy romance.
They wear a crown of bright green hair,
And give the sun a golden glare.

Sipping on breeze, they hum a tune,
In a wacky waltz with the afternoon.
Beneath their shade, a picnic may bloom,
With sandwiches flying like a cartoon.

Embracing the Horizon

Reaching out to the distant rays,
They play footsie with the ocean's waves.
With rustling leaves like laughter's cheer,
They bounce like kids when no one's near.

A guardian of dreams so sweet,
They dance around on nimble feet.
Tanning up high, a silly sight,
As seagulls laugh at their flight.

Wind-Kissed Reveries

Whispering secrets the wind has told,
Their tales unfold in shades of gold.
With fronds like arms, they wave hello,
To all the birds that dip and flow.

A rustle here, a giggle there,
Their breezy humor fills the air.
Tickling the clouds with glee so bright,
They invite each star to join the night.

Sanctuary of Shadows

In the cool nook where shadows creep,
They hold the dreams that make us leap.
With every gust, a smirk appears,
As laughter dances, shedding fears.

A board of science, a silly quiz,
Which critters chill, and which just fizz?
Their roots dug deep in sand and smiles,
Creating joy that lingers for miles.

Swaying Silhouettes

In the breeze, they wiggle and shake,
Dancing tall, like they're on a break.
With a wave, they tell silly tales,
Of sunburnt tourists and fishy gales.

Each trunk a story, every frond a joke,
They chuckle at surfers who often croak.
Underneath, picnics hide from the heat,
While ants giggle at crumbs, oh what a treat!

Coconuts drop with a plop and a splash,
Silly folks jump, and boy, do they crash!
Shadowy figures, all stumbling around,
In this leafy world, laughter's the sound.

So sway on, you silhouettes, in your green,
With every twirl, chase away the mean.
A flick of a leaf, a dance in the wind,
Life's a grand joke, let the fun begin!

Embrace of the Island Breeze

The chill in the air tickles your nose,
As the breeze arrives, anything goes!
It rustles the leaves, wears a goofy grin,
Pulls on your shorts; it's a cheeky spin!

With a smile so bright, it teases your hair,
Whispers sweet secrets, without a care.
'Yo, watch that frisbee!' it shouts with a cackle,
As you fumble and trip, a tangle, a tackle!

Flip-flops go flying, a scatter of fun,
The wind just chuckles, "Oh, isn't this run?
Let's play hide and seek with each gust I throw,
Chasing your hat; oh, you never will know!"

So come take a ride on this breezy delight,
With laughter and giggles, your spirits so light.
An embrace from the island, wild and carefree,
In this whirl of joy, just let yourself be!

The Tranquil Mirage

A vision of calm in a sandy delight,
Where pelicans dive and the sun shines bright.
Yet maybe it's just a mirage in view,
As I wade through the waves wearing one goofy shoe!

With a slice of pineapple balanced on head,
I walk like a king but feel more like Fred.
"Oh, look at me! I'm a beachside delight!"
The tide giggles softly, "Oh, what a sight!"

Every flip of a wave tells a jest that we know,
As shells tumble softly like laughter in flow.
The horizon winks, gives a playful tease,
Whispering secrets through sways of the breeze.

No worries to carry; it's all in good fun,
In this sunny land where the laughter won.
So if you catch sight of a shimmering glow,
It's probably just me, putting on a show!

Tropical Reveries

Under the sun, there's a wild paradise,
Monkeys with hats throwing coconuts that surprise!
Bursts of laughter from all around,
As silly tourists trip over the ground.

In dreams of coconuts, we dance a bit,
Our moves are so awkward, yet we never quit.
Chasing the seagulls, they tease us and fly,
"Catch me if you can!" they squawk as they cry!

A surfboard's a challenge; it wobbles in glee,
While we tumble and giggle, oh, just let it be!
Each wave is a riddle, a splash of delight,
In this tropical realm where we play day and night.

So gather your friends for this wild, funny ride,
Embrace each blunder with laughter as your guide.
In the sun's warm embrace, there's nothing but cheer,
In our tropical reveries, joy's always near!

Cosmos of the Tropics

Under the sun, my plans go awry,
I tried to surf but kissed the sky.
Flip-flops flying, laughter erupts,
Even the seagulls seem to erupt.

Coconuts roll like runaway cars,
With lopsided hats and bright, silly scars.
A limbo contest? I trip and I fall,
Who knew a dance could be such a brawl?

The lizards laugh as I try to jive,
In this tropical world, I'm barely alive.
But despite my blunders, I can't help but grin,
For every mishap feels like a win.

So here's to the joy in the chaos we bring,
With flip-flops, coconuts, and laughter that sings.
Life's a wild ride in the sun's warm embrace,
In this cosmic laugh, I find my own space.

Enchantment of the Shore

Waves come crashing, oh what a sight,
I threw my towel, but wow, what a flight!
Fish look confused, as I belly-flop down,
Even the crabs seem to stare with a frown.

Sandcastle dreams start to tumble and sway,
Mermaids giggle at my shoveling play.
I built a grand fortress; it was quite the scene,
Till a rogue wave said, 'Nope!' and wiped it all clean.

Footprints leading to nowhere but retreat,
A game of tag with the tide, oh what a feat!
My sunburn's a badge of this day's silly spree,
As I race with the seagulls—who's faster? Not me!

But there's magic in laughter and joy to be found,
Among the shells and the seaweed around.
In the warmth of the shore, I'll take my next pour,
With waves rolling in, who could ask for more?

Sun-Dappled Memories

Beneath a bright sky, I lost my cool drink,
It rumbled away faster than I could think.
Chasing its trail, I trip and I slide,
In the sunny ballet, I'm quite sure I cried.

Picnic ants decide to join in the fun,
As I round up the snacks with a swift, silly run.
Ketchup and mustard go flying about,
While the dog greets the chaos with a curious shout.

A hammock invites; I lay down with flair,
But the breeze grabs my hat; it's up in the air!
Sunglasses on, I squint with a laugh,
As my shorts get caught up in a wild grass shaft.

Yet in all of these moments, the mischief rings true,
With sun-dappled laughter and friends who are blue.
We'll toast to the disasters that dance in our sight,
For under the sun, every mishap feels right.

Kaleidoscope of Tranquil Moments

In flip-flops I wander, a shipwrecked crusade,
Avoiding the sun, I take shade in the glade.
Cocktails in hand, I toast to the breeze,
Until a coconut drops, saying, "Hey! Look at me!"

Sunset arrives, I spill my last drink,
The seagulls circle, they're really in sync.
A beach bonfire blaze that sparks in the night,
Someone shouts, "It's a barbeque! Oh, what a sight!"

We roast marshmallows and tell silly tales,
About misadventures and wacky whale trails.
With laughter exploding like stars in the dark,
In this blissful cocoon, we've found a sweet spark.

So here's to the moments that catch us off guard,
Where kooky and fun play the most splendid card.
We'll dance with the waves, in our own little way,
In this kaleidoscope dream, let's laugh through the day.

A Haven of Soft Breeze

In a hammock high, I sway with glee,
With snacks and drinks, my favorite spree.
A squirrel drops by, cheeky and bold,
Stealing my chips, oh, the tales to be told.

Whispers of wind, each gust's a tease,
A seagull squawks, 'Yo, share some cheese!'
Flip-flops flip-flap, they dance on the sand,
Who knew my shoes had such moves unplanned?

On this sunny throne, a royal decree,
That napping is ruling, call it a spree!
A crab walks by with an odd little strut,
"Fancy a race?" I shout with a nut!

With laughter and joy, I toast to this day,
In my beach kingdom, I'm here to stay.
Each wave a giggle, with sand in my hair,
Living the dream, without a single care.

Hues of Relaxation

A canvas of colors, both bright and wild,
Painting my world like an overgrown child.
Sunburned my nose, but hey, that's the way,
I'm the sun-kissed tomato, bold in my play!

A drink in my hand, umbrellas abound,
Where's the waiter? Lost, maybe in sound?
Oh wait, it's a seagull! Sipping my brew,
That rascal, I swear, a bird with a view!

The sun dips low, orange, red, and pink,
"Who needs a sofa?" is my new wink.
I'll nap on the sand, with grains stuck to me,
A beach bum aficionado, carefree and free!

To dance with the waves, oh, what a sight,
Flip-flops in hand, I twirl with delight.
Each splash a giggle, each wave a grin,
In hues of relaxation, let the fun begin!

Tides of Solitude

A quiet retreat, my slice of the sea,
Where the stars have come down just to chill with me.
A crab approaches, asking for snacks,
"Just a few chips," it boldly attacks!

Waves come a-laughing, they tickle my toes,
While laughter erupts like a soft summer prose.
The moon shines bright, a comedic light,
I wave to a fish, it feigns fright!

No worries nearby, just me and the breeze,
Mind's on vacation, it's doing the tease.
A rogue wave rolls in, a splash on my neck,
"Just my luck," I shout, dripping in wreck!

Yet here I remain, in solitude fine,
Building sandcastles, sipping on brine.
With each little giggle, a treasure expanded,
In these tides of joy, my heart is unbanded!

Embrace of the Sun's Caress

Bathing in sunshine, a warm golden hug,
My skin turns to toast, but I find it snug.
Chasing away clouds like a playful tease,
I invite in the sun, with tropical breeze!

Flip-flops do jigs, as I stroll with flair,
Passing a parrot, bold and rare.
"Can I borrow your beak?" I quip with a smile,
It squawks back, "Only if you dance for a while!"

In this radiant glow, I stretch and twirl,
A seagull conspirator, joins in my whirl.
With every step, giggles rise like foam,
In the embrace of this bliss, I've found my home.

The sun dips low, painting shadows on sand,
I chuckle at life, oh, isn't it grand?
With friends in the sea and sun on the skin,
This playful existence, let the laughter begin!

Reverie in the Tropics

Under coconut clouds so high,
The monkeys swing as seagulls fly.
Sunbathers blushing like ripe fruit,
Chasing crabs that think they're cute.

A smoothie spills with every laugh,
While surfers ride a foam-filled path.
Laughter echoes, waves come crashing,
Even the diet soda's splashing!

Sandcastles tall, then swept away,
By giggling tides that love to play.
Flip-flops lost in the sandy spree,
Dancing with joy, oh, what a scene!

With palm leaves waving, who needs plans?
We'll throw a party, invite the clams.
Dance like the sun is our DJ tonight,
In this tropical zone of pure delight!

Oasis of the Heart

Sipping juice from a hollow shell,
With a frown, I fell for that wishful spell.
The parrot squawks, he can't be right,
"Wear shades indoors, you'll shine real bright!"

A hammock swings, a gentle sway,
Dreaming of things that went astray.
My flip-flop flies, a daring feat,
Off to explore the sandy street!

With sun and fun, I lost my hat,
On a windy chase with a curious cat.
Even the lizards laugh at me,
In this sunny place where all are free!

But laughter reigns, we dance and sing,
In our hearts, we're the beach's king.
So join the mischief, come take a seat,
In the oasis where joy is sweet!

Bursting with Sunshine

Gather 'round, the sun is bright,
With sunglasses worn at a quirky height.
Grilled cheese sizzles, quite the delight,
While ants negotiate a food fight!

The breeze tickles, a playful tease,
As we struggle to catch our sneeze.
A coconut falls – oh, what a sound!
And laughter spreads all around!

Bubbles float, a frothy parade,
While beachgoers join in the charade.
Look at that crab, breaking it down,
While the sun shines bright on this silly town!

We twirl and spin in a sandy whirl,
Ignoring the fuss, enjoying each twirl.
Life's a carnival wrapped in charm,
In this sunny place where nothing feels harm!

Beneath Verdant Dreams

In the shade, the laughter flows,
Sipping juice, who really knows?
A squirrel steals a snack with glee,
While I'm left with just the spree!

Beneath the leaves, a picnic spread,
We munch on snacks until we're fed.
The ants organize their heist,
While we're too busy with our slice!

Surfboard jokes and sandy goals,
Trying hard to catch the moles.
Splashes come, all squeals and glee,
"Oh not the face!"–just let it be!

When twilight falls, and stars commence,
Who knew each day would be such fun?
Here's to the laughter, the chants, the schemes,
Living our best, beneath our dreams!

Dances in the Salted Air

Beneath the sun, I twist and sway,
Trying to dance in a funny way.
A seagull laughed, I tripped a bit,
Oh, salty air, you make me split!

My friends all join, they run and twirl,
With beach hats flying, they give a whirl.
The waves keep crashing, like claps of cheer,
As sand flies up, there's nothing to fear!

I stepped on a crab, it pinched my toe,
I leapt and yelped, oh where'd he go?
We laughed till we fell on the soft warm shore,
That crab knows how to dance, we need to learn more!

The palm fronds wave as if they know,
Our silly moves steal the whole show.
With each funny stumble, we burst with glee,
In the salty breeze, it's fun to be free!

Roots in the Sand

In a world of grains, I find my feet,
They wiggle and squirm, oh isn't that neat?
The grains are stubborn, they won't let go,
Roots planted deep, but why so slow?

A crab gives me side-eye, judging my stance,
While I'm trying hard to pull off a dance.
I tip on my toes, but slip on a shell,
The laughter erupts, oh this is swell!

The sun does its best, it's really no fuss,
Yet here comes a wave, making a fuss.
My roots in the sand have lost the battle,
Taking a tumble, I give a loud rattle!

With sands in my hair, I stand up proud,
Waving to strangers, oh it feels so loud.
Roots in the sand, a sight to behold,
At least I'm not boring, that's how I roll!

Echoes of the Coastal Dawn

At dawn's break, the coast starts to yawn,
I stumble outside, still wearing my fawn.
The gulls are squawking, a curious crew,
I wave to the waves, they wave back too!

The sun peek-a-boos through clouds so shy,
While I trip on driftwood, oh me, oh my!
I giggle at crabs with their funny little walk,
They strut like they're in a quirky talk!

The beach umbrella flops, like it's lost control,
I chase after it, oh what a role!
The echoes of laughter fill up the morn,
With tossed flip-flops and my hat now worn.

Seagulls and laughter, oh what a sight!
Coastal dawn echoes in pure delight.
As I shake off the sand, ready for play,
A funny adventure begins every day!

Celestial Canopies

Under the canopy, we lie flat,
Counting clouds that hover and chat.
One looks like a dog, then a gumdrop too,
As laughter spills out, we're feeling so true!

The breeze comes in, tickling our toes,
While I try to spot where the last crab goes.
Our top hats thrumming in the chill of the air,
Funny looks from strangers, I just don't care!

Stars at night drape like sparkly tinsel,
While I try to explain why I've got quite the grin.
Aliens above, are they watching us dance?
With giggles and shuffles, we give them a chance!

The celestial lights, they twinkle and jive,
Under our laughter, we truly feel alive.
In canopies high, we'll dream without end,
With a chuckle shared, where all troubles bend!

Footprints in Golden Sands

In the sand, I left my mark,
But a wave came, oh so stark!
Now it's gone, like my last snack,
Guess I'll just blame the tide's track.

Seagulls squawk, they steal my fries,
I chase them down, to my surprise!
With every step, I slip and slide,
Laughing hard, I can't abide.

The sun is shining, my skin's a glow,
But the ice cream melts, oh no, oh no!
I run to catch it, but fall instead,
Now I'm a mess, but I'm well fed!

I build a castle, tall and grand,
And wave hello with a crumbly hand.
A kid knocks it over, oh what a scene,
At least I got sand in my protein!

Canopy of Serenity

Beneath the leaves, I take a nap,
But a squirrel decides to rap!
He's chattering loud, it's quite the show,
I wake up grumpy, but off he'll go.

The breeze whispers funny little tunes,
While I sway, dreaming of balloons.
I try to dance, trip on a root,
Now I'm tangled up in my own boot!

Lemons fall from hanging boughs,
I catch one, and take a bow.
But lemon juice goes in my eye,
I see a rainbow, oh my, oh my!

Clouds drift by, they look like sheep,
I giggle, but it's just too deep.
Dreams float up, and then they're gone,
I chase them but I'm already drawn!

The Dance of Fronds

Fronds are swinging, what a sight,
I join the dance, feeling light.
But a gust takes me for a ride,
Now I'm twirling, with giggles wide!

The sun shines down, it's got a grin,
I twirl and spin, let the fun begin!
But as I leap, I trip on grass,
Dancing's great, but I'm out of gas!

Little critters join my show,
A crab slides in, in a quick tempo.
We dance together, what a crew,
But oops, he clicked, and away he flew!

A finale tumbles, down I go,
But laughter lingers, stealing the show.
With each mishap, I rise to gleam,
In this wild waltz, oh how I beam!

Swaying to the Ocean's Lullaby

Ocean sings a funky beat,
I sway and shuffle, move my feet.
But a crab pinches, oh what a tease,
I dance away, aiming for ease.

Waves crash down, splash on my face,
I wipe it off, it's all a race!
Seashells gather, all in a line,
I trip on one — now, ain't that fine?

Birds above are making quirks,
They seem to dance, with silly jerks.
I try to join, but lose my way,
In this party, I'm just a cliché!

The moon peeks out, gives a wink,
As I twirl, I start to sink.
With every bob, I lifeguard my snack,
Swaying away, just don't look back!

Journey to the Horizon

My hat flew off into the sea,
A seagull claimed it, wild and free.
I waved goodbye with a fruity drink,
As the waves laughed hard, I could only blink.

A crab danced close, stealing my fries,
I chuckled loud at his gluttonous guise.
Will he share them with his crusty crew?
Oh, life at the shore, it's a comical view!

I chased the tide, slipped, took a dive,
The ocean teased, "Look, he's still alive!"
With sand in my shorts and a grin on my face,
I spread my arms, embracing the space.

As the sun set low, I dreamed away,
About things that could happen if crabs could play.
Tomorrow's a mystery, with laughter to find,
In the humorous dance where the sea meets the mind.

Treetop Whispering Tales

Up in the branches, the monkeys swing,
Finding my snacks, they're quite the king!
They chatter and chatter, a funny affair,
Do they think within leaves, all worries are rare?

The wind told secrets, rustling the leaves,
While I held my sides, oh, how it believes!
Squirrels were plotting a nut-gathering scheme,
While visions of acorns danced in my dream.

A wise old owl snoozes, then wakes up to say,
"Life's just a hoot when you laugh every day!"
With fruit on my head, I strutted around,
"Who knew tree tops had comedy abound?"

The breeze threw in some puns, what a delight,
I guess the tall plants know how to write!
With giggles and snickers, we basked in the sun,
This treetop adventure has just begun!

Echoes of the Coastal Heart

The clam shells clink like a jazzy band,
Salsa dancing on the shifting sand.
As I joined in with my awkward moves,
The fish all laughed; oh, what a groove!

Seashells whispered of secrets so grand,
Like the time I tripped, oh, isn't life planned?
A dolphin winked, plotting a splash,
"Come on in, let's make a big splash!"

Crabs were my judges, with claws held up high,
"Your rhythm is weak, but oh my, oh my!"
With a bow and a grin, I twirled with grace,
In the echoes of laughter, I found my place.

As the tides rolled in, bringing tales anew,
The beach was our stage, a comical view.
With each giddy moment, the sun dipped low,
We danced by the shore, letting laughter flow.

Sanctuary of the Swaying Heart

Under the boughs, where the shadows play,
I overheard a parrot gossiping away.
"Have you seen the raccoon with the crazy hat?
He thinks he can dance, but, oh, he is flat!"

Bees buzzed in circles, a dance of delight,
While ants formed a conga, oh what a sight!
The frogs held auditions with croaks of pure glee,
For the best performance, just wait and just see!

In this grove of giggles, life dances along,
With melodies played by a hilarity song.
Grab a friend, share a laugh, wear a silly grin,
In this sanctuary, we always win!

As the sun took a bow, the night joined the fun,
With fireflies twinkling, the laughter begun.
With swaying hearts and funny little dreams,
We found joy forever, or so, it seems!

Journey to Paradise

With flip-flops on I float away,
Dreaming of a sandy bay.
The seagulls laugh, they steal my fries,
While I chase my dreams beneath the skies.

A coconut drops, it lands on my hat,
I shake my fist at a sunbathing cat.
But who can frown in this sunny light?
I dance with shadows, oh what a sight!

The ice cream melts but I'm feeling fine,
I trade it for a piña colada line.
The waves invite me with a silly cheer,
Come hop on board, there's nothing to fear!

In paradise, my worries flee,
With laughter echoing from the sea.
So let me sail where the sunbeams play,
And turn my troubles into a cabana ballet!

Serenity Amongst the Fronds

Under fronds, I hear a tune,
A funky beat that makes me swoon.
The breeze giggles, waves will tease,
As I wiggle my toes with utmost ease.

A gecko struts, he's got some flair,
He's wearing shades, I swear it's rare.
They call him Lou, the lizard king,
In our leafy world, all vibes take wing.

I sip my drink, it spills on my lap,
The fronds just laugh, oh what a trap!
With fruit on my head, I join the dance,
Waving to crabs who refuse to prance.

Here in this haven, life's bizarre,
I'm clumsy but happy, like a shining star.
The sunset paints a playful scene,
Amongst the fronds, I feel like a queen!

Lullaby of the Shoreline

The waves hum softly, a cheeky tune,
As sandcastles crumble under the moon.
A crab plays tag with a lost flip-flop,
Grinning wide, it's fun till you stop!

Seagulls sing, "Get your own bread!"
While I dream of tacos in my bed.
Oh, how the ocean whispers and sways,
In lullabies that last whole days!

My beach chair squeaks, it groans in pain,
As I nap with sunscreen on my brain.
But what's that sound? Oh, just my snores,
A symphony of laughs from the ocean floors!

So let me drift on this sandy shore,
With laughter echoing forevermore.
As tides remind me, 'Life's a play!'
I'm the star of this silly ballet!

The Spirit of Sun-Kissed Isles

In sun-kissed shades, I strut with glee,
Convinced I'm the funniest fish in the sea.
A beach ball bounces, it smacks my nose,
But I just grin, and wiggle my toes.

There's a parrot who tells absurd jokes,
While iguanas dance to the rhythm of croaks.
They parade and sway, in riotous cheer,
I can't help but chuckle; the vibe's crystal clear.

The sun bows low on the horizon bright,
As I trip over my towel, what a sight!
With laughter spilling like spilled lemonade,
The spirit of joy will never fade.

So let's toast with coconuts, let's raise a cheer,
To silly moments that bring us near.
Life's a holiday, with giggles at heart,
In this sunny paradise, we'll never part!

Reverberations of Time Beneath the Canopy

In the shade, where I nap,
Tropical birds do a tap dance.
Chasing dreams on a warm breeze,
Life's silly at a glance.

Coconuts fall with a thud,
While I sip my coconut milk.
A squirrel steals my sandwich toast,
They think they're so smooth and silk.

The sun blinks through each leaf,
Waves of laughter and sun rays.
My hat flies high, oh dear me!
It's a hat-trick sort of day!

Underneath the vibrant fronds,
The sand tickles my bare feet.
I dance and trip, what a laugh,
Oh, life's simply a treat!

Whispers of the Oasis

A breeze brings tales of the past,
As lizards wiggle and prance.
My drink's not mixed just right,
But hey, let's give it a chance!

The sun's a mischievous prankster,
Winking through the green leaves.
I'm stuck in a hammock, quite stuck,
But giggles bring sweet reprieves.

Lost flip-flops, where could they roam?
Under a laughing lizard's gaze.
I'd chase them if I weren't so comfy,
In my sun-soaked daze!

Giggling palms dance in the breeze,
Mimicking my goofy sway.
Let's toast with fizzy laughter,
As another day fades away!

Shadows of the Tropics

Under the leaves, I make a wish,
For never-ending beach days.
The shadows play peek-a-boo,
With the sun's glistening rays.

A crab scuttles with a grin,
Thinking he owns the shore.
I try to walk by it cool,
But trips leave me wanting more!

With sunscreen slathered like a paste,
I walk like a penguin, so sly.
Fellow tourists chuckle away,
As I wave my arms, "Oh my!"

Twilight blooms in orange hues,
In this mishap-filled boredom.
I'll remember these silly hours,
On my lighthearted kingdom.

Beneath Sunlit Canopies

Beneath the leaves, I play hide-and-seek,
With shadows far and wide.
Goldfish float in coconut bowls,
Laughing at my silly stride.

A chubby iguana yawns loud,
As I try to catch my breath.
He seems wise, giving me looks,
Like, "Here's your life, don't fret!"

The breeze tosses my beach hat high,
I become its cheering fan.
I chase it through the cheery sands,
Like a crazy, happy man.

At dusk, we gather, all of us,
Laughing over blunders made.
Each story shared, more laughter grows,
In this joy-filled escapade!